# THE BEST OF ABBA

©Michael Ochs Archives/Corbis

ISBN 978-1-4234-8758-6

HAL•LEONARD®
CORPORATION

7777 W. BLUEMOUND RD. P.O. BOX 13819 MILWAUKEE, WI 53213

Visit Hal Leonard Online at
www.halleonard.com

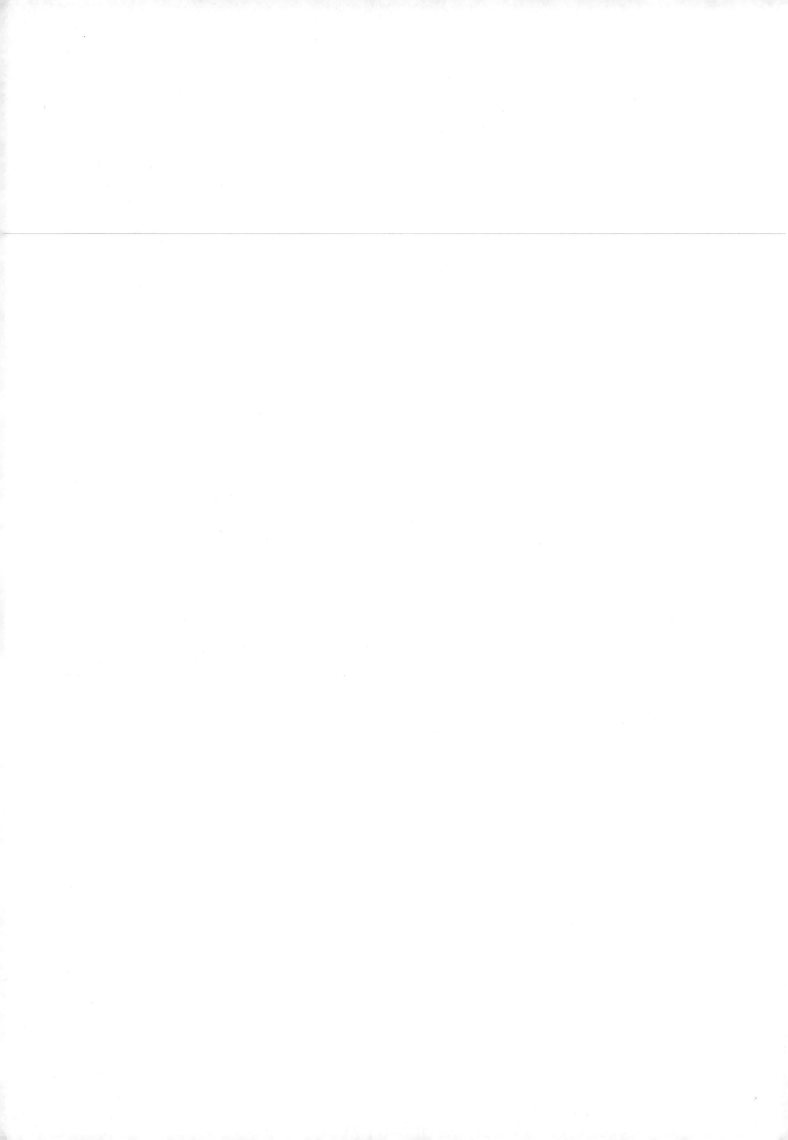

# THE BEST OF ABBA

# ANGEL EYES

Words and Music by BENNY ANDERSSON
and BJÖRN ULVAEUS

* *Recorded a half step lower*

N.C.

**Repeat and Fade**

# CHIQUITITA

Words and Music by BENNY ANDERSSON,
BJÖRN ULVAEUS and BUDDY MARY MAC-CLUSKEY

Chi - qui - ti - ta, tell me what's wrong,
truth,
down,

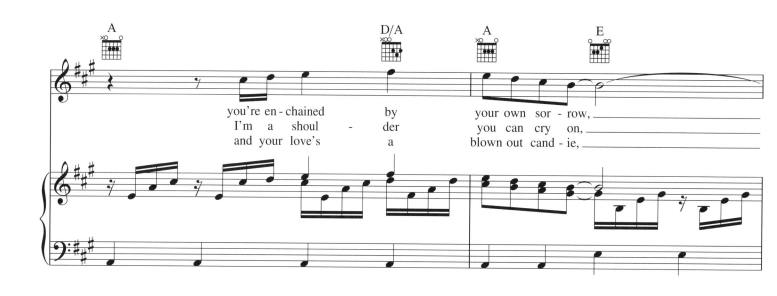

you're en - chained by your own sor - row,
I'm a shoul - der you can cry on,
and your love's a blown out cand - ie,

in _____ your eyes there is no hope
your _____ best friend, I'm the one you
all _____ is gone and it seems too

# DANCING QUEEN

Words and Music by BENNY ANDERSSON,
BJÖRN ULVAEUS and STIG ANDERSON

# EAGLE

Words and Music by
BENNY ANDERSSON
and BJÖRN ULVAEUS

They came fly-in' from far a-way, ___
As all good friends we talk all night, ___

now I'm un-der their spell,
and we fly wing to wing,

I love hear-ing the
I have ques-tions and

sto-ries that they ___ tell,
they know ev-'ry - thing,

22

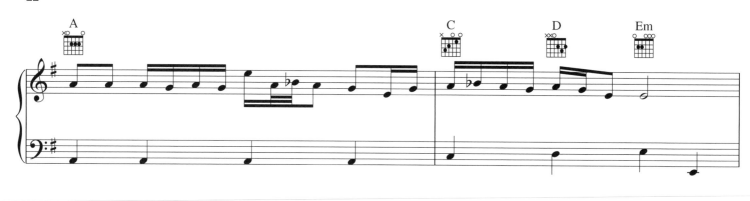

And I dream I'm an ea - gle,

and I dream I can spread my wings. Fly - in' high, high, I'm a

# DOES YOUR MOTHER KNOW

Words and Music by BENNY ANDERSSON
and BJÖRN ULVAEUS

**Medium Pop**

in your face that your feel - ings are driv - ing you wild, ___ ah, ___
what you mean when you give me a flash of that smile, ___ ah, ___

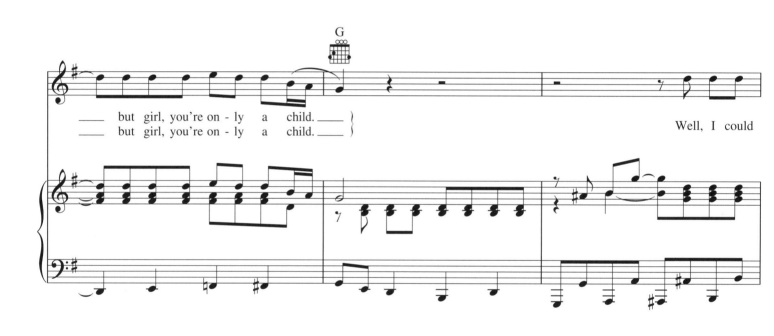

___ but girl, you're on - ly a child. ___
___ but girl, you're on - ly a child. ___

Well, I could

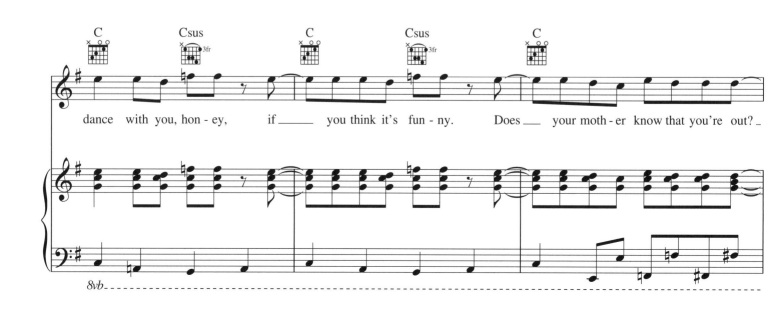

dance with you, hon - ey, if ___ you think it's fun - ny. Does ___ your moth - er know that you're out? _

8vb - - - - - - - - - - - - - - - - - - - - - - - - - - - - - - - - - -

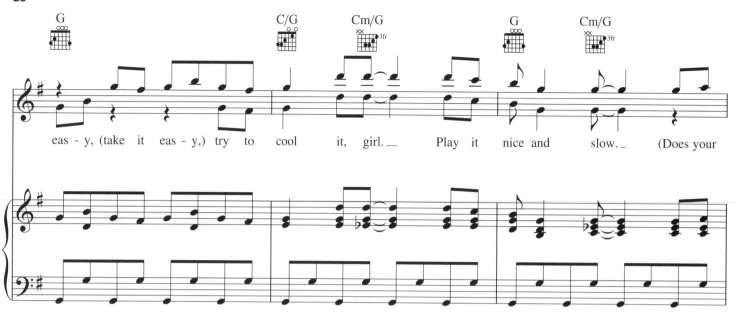

eas-y, (take it eas-y,) try to cool it, girl.__ Play it nice and slow.__ (Does your

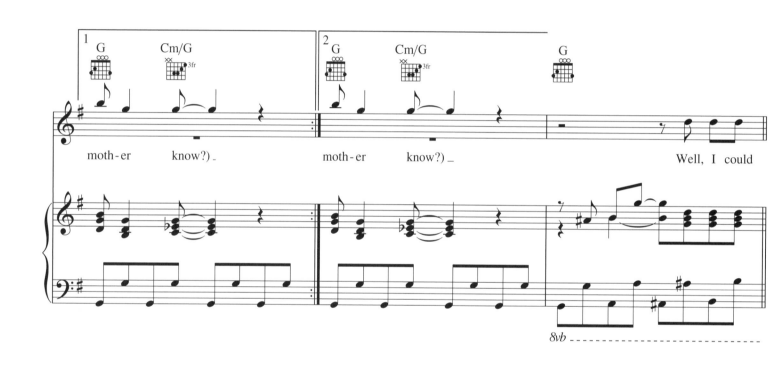

moth-er know?)__      moth-er know?)__      Well, I could

dance with you, hon-ey, if ___ you think it's fun-ny.  Does ___ your moth-er know that you're out?__

And I could chat with you, ba - by, flirt___ a lit - tle may - be. Does___

**Repeat and Fade**

___ your moth - er know that you're out? _____ Well, I could

**Optional Ending**

___ your moth - er know that you're out? _____

# FERNANDO

Words and Music by BENNY ANDERSSON,
BJÖRN ULVAEUS and STIG ANDERSON

In the fi - re - light, Fer - nan - do,
I was so a - fraid, Fer - nan - do,
Can you hear the drums, Fer - nan - do?

you were hum - ming to your - self and soft - ly strum - ming your gui -
we were young and full of life and none of us pre - pared to
Do you still re - call the fright - ful night we crossed the Ri - o

tar.
die.
Grande?

I could hear the dis - tant drums and sounds of bu - gle calls were
And I'm not a - shamed to say the roar of guns and can - nons
I can see it in your eyes how proud you were to fight for

# GIMME! GIMME! GIMME!
## (A Man After Midnight)

Words and Music by BENNY ANDERSSON
and BJÖRN ULVAEUS

**Moderate Rock**

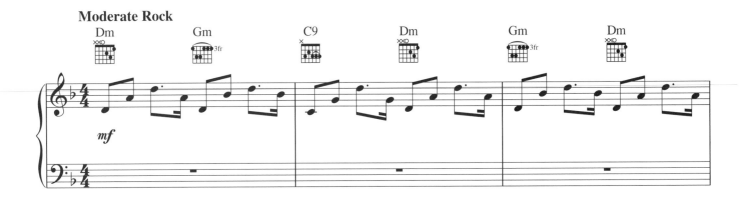

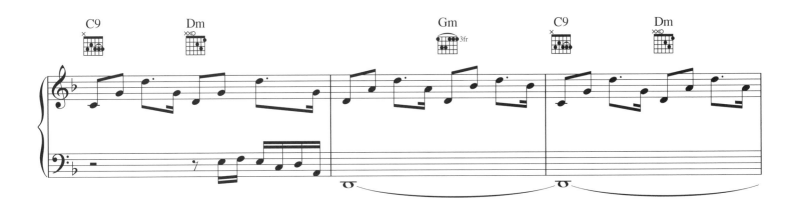

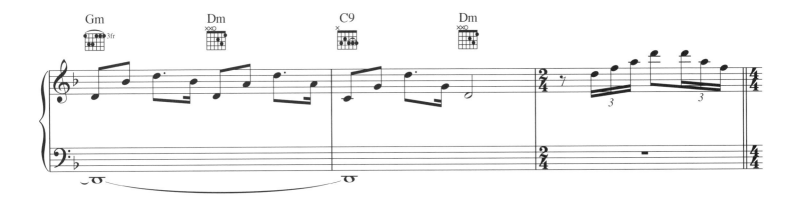

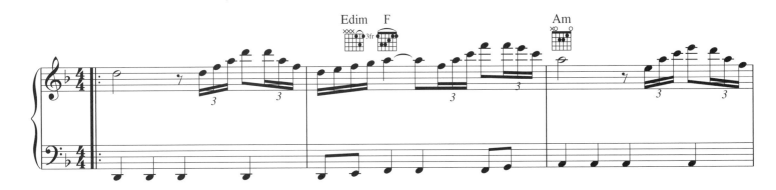

Half past twelve and I'm watch - in' the late __ show in my flat all a - lone. __ How I
Mov - ie stars find the end of the rain - bow with a for - tune to win. __ It's too

hate to spend the eve - ning on my own. Au - tumn winds blow - in'
dif - ferent from the world __ I'm liv - in' in. Tired of T - V I

# I HAVE A DREAM

Words and Music by BENNY ANDERSSON
and BJÖRN ULVAEUS

# HONEY, HONEY

Words and Music by BENNY ANDERSSON,
BJÖRN ULVAEUS and STIG ANDERSON

# I DO I DO I DO I DO I DO

Words and Music by BENNY ANDERSSON,
BJÖRN ULVAEUS and STIG ANDERSON

# KNOWING ME, KNOWING YOU

Words and Music by BENNY ANDERSSON,
BJÖRN ULVAEUS and STIG ANDERSON

58

# LAY ALL YOUR LOVE ON ME

Words and Music by BENNY ANDERSSON
and BJÖRN ULVAEUS

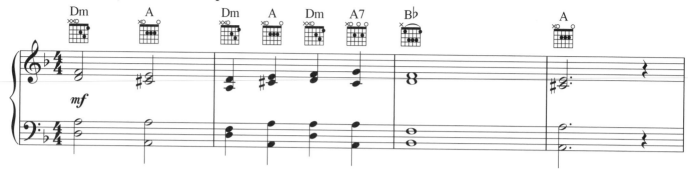

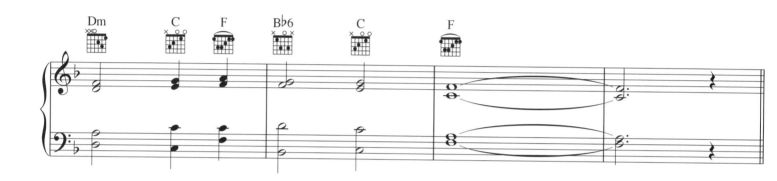

I was-n't jeal - ous be - fore we met,
It was like shoot - ing a sit - ting duck,
I've had a few lit - tle love af - fairs,

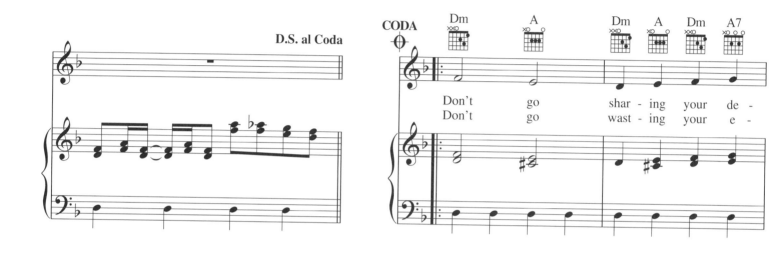

D.S. al Coda

CODA

Don't    go    shar - ing    your    de -
Don't    go    wast - ing    your    e -

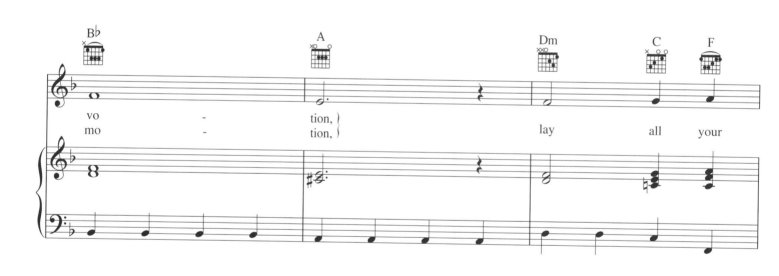

vo -       tion, }
mo -       tion, }                    lay    all    your

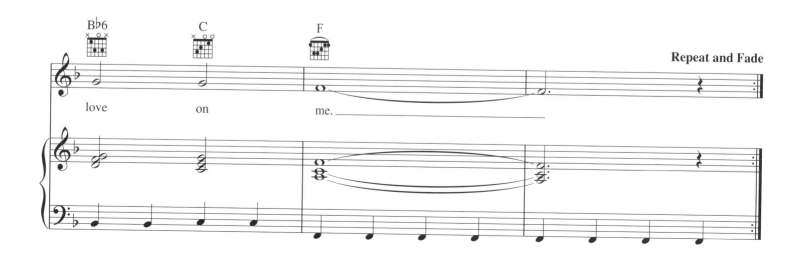

Repeat and Fade

love       on       me. _____

# S.O.S.

Words and Music by BENNY ANDERSSON,
BJÖRN ULVAEUS and STIG ANDERSON

how can I __ car - ry on?

# MAMMA MIA

Words and Music by BENNY ANDERSSON,
BJÖRN ULVAEUS and STIG ANDERSON

# MONEY, MONEY, MONEY

Words and Music by BENNY ANDERSSON
and BJÖRN ULVAEUS

I work all night, I work all day to   pay the bills I have to pay. _

Mon-ey, mon-ey, mon-ey     must be fun-ny     in a rich man's world. _

Mon-ey, mon-ey, mon-ey     al-ways sun-ny

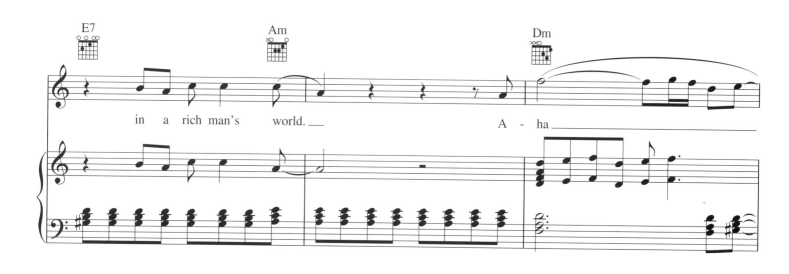

in a rich man's world. _     A - ha _____

# OUR LAST SUMMER

Words and Music by BENNY ANDERSSON
and BJÖRN ULVAEUS

88

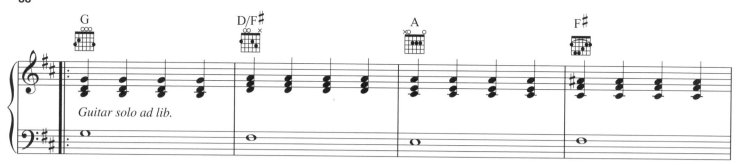

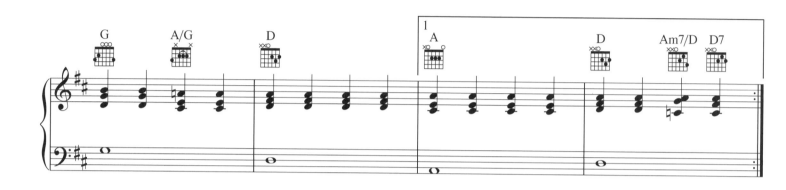

And now you're work-in' in a bank, a fam'ly man, a foot-ball

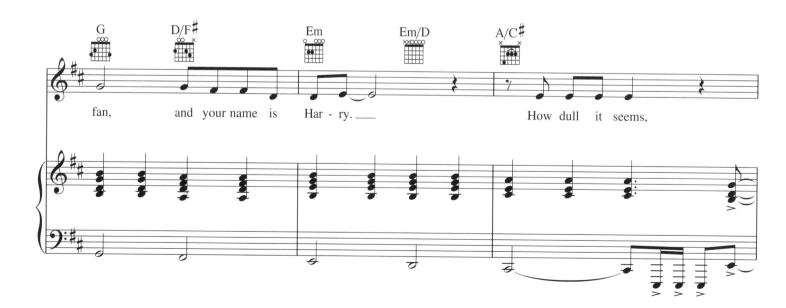

fan, and your name is Har - ry. ___ How dull it seems,

# RING, RING

Words and Music by BENNY ANDERSSON,
BJÖRN ULVAEUS, STIG ANDERSON,
NEIL SEDAKA and PHIL CODY

**Moderately fast**

I was sit - ting by ___ the phone, ___ I was
here and now ___ you're gone, ___ hey, did

wait - ing all ___ a - lone, ___ ba - by, by my - self ___ I sit and
I do some - thing wrong? ___ I just can't be - lieve ___ that I could

wait and won - der a - bout you. ___ It's a
be so bad - ly mis - ta - ken. ___ Was it

# SUMMER NIGHT CITY

Words and Music by BENNY ANDERSSON
and BJÖRN ULVAEUS

**Moderately**

Sum-mer night cit - y, _____

sum-mer night cit - y. _____ Wait-ing for the sun-rise soul-

# SUPER TROUPER

Words and Music by BENNY ANDERSSON
and BJÖRN ULVAEUS

Su - per Trou - per beams are gon - na blind __ me

but I won't feel blue

like I al - ways

do, _____ 'cause some - where in the crowd __ there's you.

# WATERLOO

Words and Music by BENNY ANDERSSON,
BJÖRN ULVAEUS and STIG ANDERSON

# TAKE A CHANCE ON ME

Words and Music by BENNY ANDERSSON
and BJÖRN ULVAEUS

**Moderate Dance beat**

If you change your mind, _____ I'm the first in line. _____

_____ Hon-ey, I'm still free, _____ take a chance on me. _____ If you need me, let _____

_____ me know. Gon-na be a-round, _____ if you got no place _____ to go when you're

# THANK YOU FOR THE MUSIC

Words and Music by BENNY ANDERSSON
and BJÖRN ULVAEUS

# VOULEZ-VOUS

Words and Music by BENNY ANDERSSON
and BJÖRN ULVAEUS

**Disco**

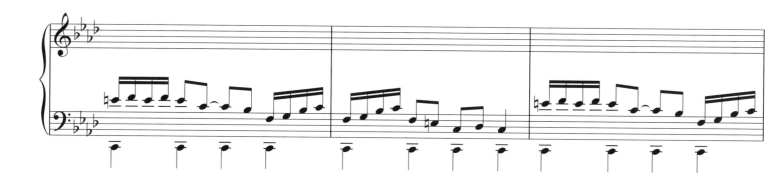

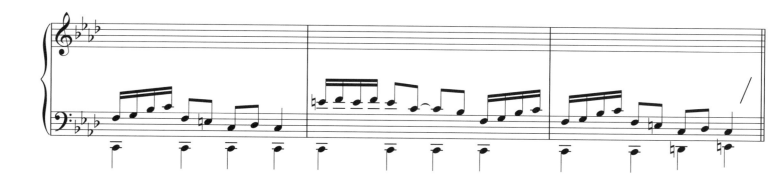

# WHEN ALL IS SAID AND DONE

Words and Music by BENNY ANDERSSON
and BJÖRN ULVAEUS

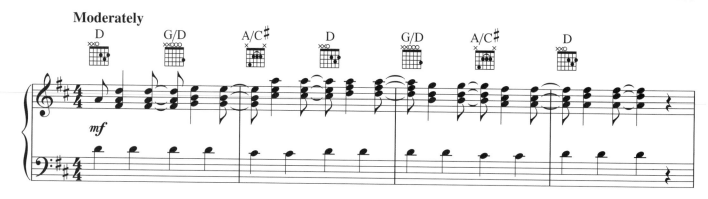

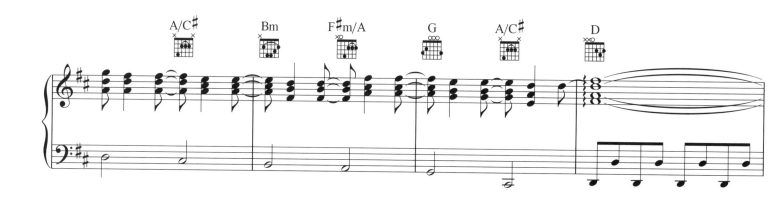

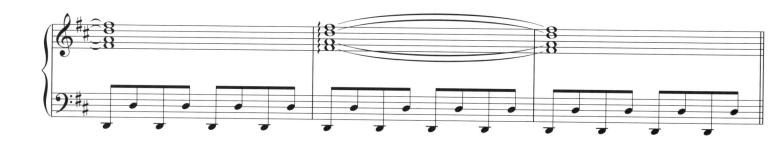

Here's to us, ___ one more toast ___ and then ___ we'll pay ___ the bill.
In our lives ___ we have walked ___ some strange ___ and lone - ly treks,
It's so strange ___ when you're down ___ and ly - ing on ___ the floor ___

128

nei - ther you _ nor I'm _ to blame _ when all _ is said _ and done. _
Nei - ther you _ nor I'm _ to blame _ when all _ is said _ and done. _
There's no hur - ry an - y - more _ when all _ is said _ and done. _

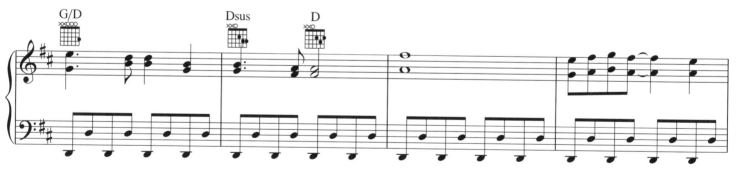

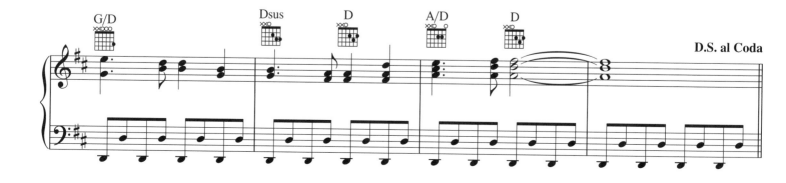

# THE WINNER TAKES IT ALL

Words and Music by BENNY ANDERSSON
and BJÖRN ULVAEUS

I don't wan - na talk
arms
kiss
talk

a - bout things we've gone through,
think - ing I be - longed there,
like I used to kiss you,
though it's hurt - ing
if it makes you feel sad,
does it feel the
and I un - der -

To Coda

no more ace to play.
play - ing by the rules.
rules must be o - beyed.
no self con - fi - dence.

The win - ner takes it
The gods may throw a
The judg - es will de -
The win - ner takes it

all,
dice,
cide,

the los - er stand - ing small
their minds as cold as ice,
the likes of me a - bide,

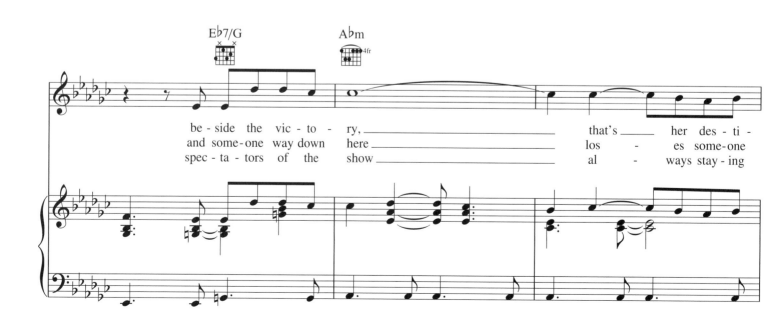

be - side the vic - to - ry, _____ that's _____ her des - ti -
and some - one way down here _____ los - es some - one
spec - ta - tors of the show _____ al - ways stay - ing